Lighthouses and Living Along the Florida Gulf Coast

by *Best Wishes William Roberts*

William Roberts

authorHOUSE™

1663 LIBERTY DRIVE, SUITE 200
BLOOMINGTON, INDIANA 47403
(800) 839-8640
WWW.AUTHORHOUSE.COM

First published by AuthorHouse 07/11/05

ISBN: 1-4208-4898-4 (sc)

Library of Congress Control Number: 2005904141

Printed in the United States of America
Bloomington, Indiana

This book is printed on acid-free paper.

Table of Contents

Dedication and Foreword

I am proud to dedicate this book to the memories of Walter Andrew Roberts, Sr., Walter Andrew Roberts, Jr., and Walter Andrew Roberts III and to all lighthouse keepers for their dedication and devotion to the United States Lighthouse Service and service to others.

The Roberts' dedication and devotion began in 1894 when grandfather, Walter Andrew Roberts, Sr., was assigned as 1st Assistant Keeper at the Cape Saint George Lighthouse at Apalachicola and that dedication and devotion continued for over fifty-eight years and three generations until 1952 when my father retired from the United States Coast Guard at the Saint Joseph Rear Range Lighthouse in Port Saint Joe, Florida.

My Thanks

Thanks to my wife, Verner, for her patience throughout all this process, to Joe Harrison and Mike Mitchell for their foresight and encouragement for this book, to Charlotte Maddox Pierce for her courage to give me an opportunity to express my love for lighthouses and the boosts along the way, to Barbara Revell for her sincere interest in my presentations and her efforts to lift my morale, to Beverly Douds for her research help.

My thanks to all of you, the dedicated lighthouse people who volunteered information, offered research help and friends that just gave me encouragement every so often.

My special thanks to Darrel, Diane, Kris and all the AuthorHouse Design Consultants, for their expertise and guidance in bringing my manuscript from words and pictures to a wonderful family portrait and their roles in making my lifetime dream come true.

William C. Roberts

Three Generations of Keepers Of The Lighthouses

Walter Andrew Roberts, Sr.

Walter Andrew Roberts, Jr.

Walter Andrew Roberts III

Introduction

For hundreds of years, lighthouses have served as beacons in the night for both navigators and those lost at sea. Countless ships and lives were saved thanks to their warning lights. Lighthouses are the oldest kind of navigational aid used by man. In the most primitive form, they were nothing more than fires lighted at the entrance of a harbor to guide the ships home or warn sailors of dangerous shoals. Some lighthouses, equipped with powerful Fresnel lenses, were visible as far as 25 miles out to sea. But, with new methods of navigation, many lighthouses have become obsolete and no longer act as lighted sentinels along dangerous shores.

The oldest recorded lighthouse was Pharos of Alexandria, Egypt, which was erected about 280 B.C. It stood more than 350 feet tall until an earthquake completely destroyed it in the 1300s.

The first lighthouse, built in America was the Boston Harbor Light on Little Brewster Island in Boston Harbor, was first lighted on 14 September 1716, and is the only active lighthouse in the United States that is still manned by the U. S. Coast Guard. The tallest masonry lighthouse in the United States is the Cape Hatteras Lighthouse on the Outer Banks of North Carolina. It measured at 207.49 feet and was built 1,600 feet from edge of the Atlantic Ocean but was recently moved 2,900 feet inland at an estimated cost of $10 million dollars.

The most famous American lighthouse and the first lighthouse to use electricity is the Statue of Liberty in New York harbor. From its opening day 1886 until its deactivation as a lighthouse in 1902, its torch carried an electric light that was visible for 24 miles.

The 200th anniversary of the creation of the Lighthouse Service was celebrated in 1989. It was created on August 7, 1789 by the 9th Act of the first Congress. There were never more than 850 lighthouses in operation at once, although, about 1,500 were constructed in this country over the years, the hey-day being about 1910. In 1883, there were more than 2,200-lighted navigational aids of one kind or another throughout the United States. Although the Lighthouse Service was not a military organization, the light keepers wore uniforms. This practice began in 1883, when the Lighthouse Service issued a Directive that prescribed both dress and fatigue uniforms and required keepers to wear one or the other on all proper occasions. This Directive also outlined aspects of keepers' responsibilities, e.g., rules of conduct, hiring requirements and duties, namely, requirements to clean the stations, record daily activities and log daily weather conditions. In addition, the keepers were required to see the oil lamps were filled, wicks trimmed, lenses cleaned and polished. Building and tower maintenance were levied on the keepers, however, the Directive did exclude women keepers from this duty. The district inspectors were required to check these items on their quarterly inspections.

Lighthouses come in many shapes and sizes. This evolution has taken centuries and was influenced by technological change. Twelve lighthouses were built in the United States before the Constitution transferred lighthouse control from the states to the federal government. No two were constructed from the same set of plans and all were built from local materials. Therefore, it is no surprise that no two were alike. Examination of the one, which remains, Sandy Hook, New Jersey, and the evidence of those, which have not survived, reveals that these did share some common features. Those early lighthouses were constructed of wood or stone. Those built of wood eventually fell victim to fire. The stone towers were built by piling one stone on top of another and held together by mortar. The walls contained no additional support so they had to be tapered as they rose. This enabled the base to support the increasing weight prevented the tower from becoming unstable so the higher the tower, the thicker the tower had to be at the base.

Life on the stations could be filled with loneliness and monotony but the Service allowed married keepers to have their families live with them. In another effort to help the keepers expand their minds, the Service provided portable libraries of about fifty volumes; the books were shipped in cases "so constructed that they make a rather neat appearance". These volumes were exchanged whenever the supply tender brought supplies to the stations, usually every three to six months.

In 1939, the United States Coast Guard assumed command of all lighthouses, beacons and aids to navigation. The lighthouse keepers were given the options to retire, stay until retirement or enlist in the Coast Guard. Many of the keepers opted to enlist in the Coast Guard and spent their remaining years tending the lights and beacons.

Chapter One

THE BEGINNING:
THE FIRST GENERATION DEDICATION STARTS HERE...
Cape Saint George Lighthouse, Apalachicola, Florida

Cape Saint George Lighthouse
CA 1905
Florida State Archives

Walter Andrew Roberts, Sr
Roberts Family Collection

For generations past, our families have been tied to the sea. Way back in the 1700s, relatives were plying their trades as sailors, captains and seafaring people in and around Key West, Florida, and the Bahamas.

Our first connection with manning of lighthouses befell to my grandfather, Walter Andrew Roberts, Senior. Walter was born in Key

1

West on February 22, 1871; his father, William, was a seaman sailing the Atlantic Ocean and the Gulf of Mexico and his mother, Ann Elizabeth Archer, was the daughter of Benjamin Archer, Jr., a local blacksmith, son of Benjamin Archer, Sr., plantation owner and trader in the Bahamas.[1]

On June 13, 1894, Walter was appointed 1st Assistant Keeper at the Cape Saint George Lighthouse, Apalachicola, Florida, and trimmed his first wick at the age of 23 years.

The Saint George Lighthouse, located on Little Saint George Island, blinked on in 1833. The tower rose 65 feet and held 13 lamps intensified by reflectors. This lighthouse was built at West Pass but many mariners coming from the east could not see the light until they were in shallow water so the lighthouse was removed.

In 1847, a new lighthouse was built two miles from the original site on Cape Saint George. It lasted four years before being toppled by a storm. The third lighthouse, 72 feet high was built in 1852 using bricks and materials from the previous lighthouse; although damaged during the Civil War and washed by many hurricanes and storms, still stands today.

The lighthouse station consisted of a group of buildings – the light tower, small oil storage building near the tower, keeper's and assistant keeper's dwellings, laundry building, three large water cisterns, stable, chicken house and two outhouses. The dwellings, cisterns and laundry building were bounded on the west and north sides by white picket fences and on the south and east sides by hurricane fences to protect the station from the Gulf of Mexico tides.

At the station, the keeper and his family lived in the large three bedroom one-story frame house. There was a porch all around the house and a connecting kitchen. The assistant keeper's house was two-storied,

---

[1] 1870 U. S. Census, Key West, Monroe County, Florida, 24 June 1870, Page 25, Item 8.

with a brick lower floor with connecting kitchen and a frame upper story.

The Porter name was prominent in the area, Edward G. Porter, son of Mary Tibbett Slater and Richard Gibbs Porter, became identified with Little Saint George Island. Edward had transferred from Cape San Blas Lighthouse and became so fond of Little Saint George Island that he bought 1,515 acres of land in 1894 and built a cottage on the island and hired Miss Ola Rhodes to teach a school. Ten students, of whom six were members of his family, attended the school; the other four belonged to the family of Walter Roberts, the assistant keeper.[2] Mr. Porter's death in 1913 cut short his plans to build vacation cottages on the island.

Walter married Ada Florence McNeil, daughter of John B. McNeil and Emily Louise McNeil of Apalachicola. Walter and Ada Florence were parents of five children:

Myra Roberts	b. 1894	d. 1956
Walter Andrew Roberts, Jr.	b. 1896	d. 1977
Claude John Roberts	b. 1899	d. 1918
Maude Roberts	b. 1904	d.
Minnie Roberts	b. 1912	d. 1966

Walter served as assistant keeper under Keeper Porter until August 20, 1902, when he transferred to the Cape San Blas Lighthouse near Port Saint Joe, Florida, and served seven years as keeper. In April 1909, he returned to the Cape Saint George Lighthouse and served three years as 1st Assistant Keeper after a swapping of positions with Assistant Keeper William J. Knickmeyer.[3]

---

[2] Rogers, William (1986), <u>Outposts On The Gulf,</u> Pensacola, Florida, University of West Florida Press.

[3] The Star, Star Publishing Company, Port Saint Joe, Gulf County, Florida, dated January 24, 2002, "<u>Lighthouse Keeper's Son Sheds Light On Coast History</u>".

Upon retirement from the lighthouse service in 1912, Walter moved his family to Apalachicola. He operated the Porter family meat market for several years and later worked at the post office in Apalachicola. Grandfather Roberts died in Apalachicola on August 14, 1932 and was buried in Magnolia Cemetery. Grandmother Roberts died in Apalachicola on November 5, 1946 and was buried beside grandfather.

Keeper Edward G. Porter
Pearl Porter Marshall Collection

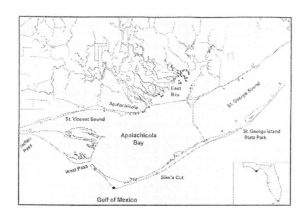

The Islands Around Apalachicola, Florida

St. Vincent Island   St. George Island   Dog Island

Chapter Two

Cape San Blas Lighthouse, Port Saint Joe, Florida

Roberts Family Collection

In 1842, the Apalachicola Chamber of Commerce sent a memorial to Congress referred to committee on December 28, 1842, recommending a lighthouse at Cape San Blas, calling the lighthouse at St. Joseph Point "a harbor light and in no degree useful to commerce, as that port is entirely abandoned for commercial purposes. The loss of life and property has been considerable. During the past year, the brig, Garland, cargo and several lives were lost on Cape San Blas". Reference: //79, v26, page 584. In 1844, several recommendations were received from vessel masters asking for a coastal lighthouse at Cape San Blas, most of them stating that the lighthouse at St. Joseph Bay was pretty useless.[4] Cape San Blas Lighthouse is located just east of Port Saint Joe on a 750-

acre piece of land that juts out into the hurricane prone Gulf of Mexico from the crook of the narrow St. Joseph peninsular.

The Cape has the dubious honor of having the most towers constructed (4) and the most towers destroyed (3) than any other Florida lighthouse site. Today, all that remains of the first brick lighthouse built in April 1848 to warn mariners of the sandy shoals extending six miles off the cape is under about 20 feet of water and about one-half mile in the gulf. A second tower lighted in November 1855; this tower fell during a hurricane ten months later. The third lighthouse was erected and a new third-order lens was lighted on May 1, 1859. The Confederate Army burned all wooden buildings including the keepers' quarters but the tower survived; the Confederate Lighthouse Superintendent had removed the lens and clockwork prior to the attack on the lighthouse. The tower was relighted on July 15, 1866 and four years later in 1870, the Gulf of Mexico was washing the base of the tower during gales and later that year the tower stood in eight feet of water.

On days of calm seas, the keepers rowed to the tower to light the lantern but in rough weather and high seas, a sixth-order fixed light was hoisted on a pole onshore, visible eleven miles into the gulf. Its position is now marked on nautical charts as an obstruction in twenty feet of water.

The fourth tower was lighted on June 30, 1885; the iron skeletal tower that overlooks the cape today was lighted using the old third-order lens from the third tower. However, the erosion continued and in only three years that distance was shortened to two hundred feet. In 1894, a hurricane again placed this tower and the Cape Saint George Lighthouse tower in the surf and wrecked the keeper's dwelling.

In April 1896, the light was temporarily discontinued as plans to dismantle the tower and move it to a new location on Black's Island in St. Joseph Bay. The government allocated funds for the move but the tower was temporarily stabilized on its original site and the lens was

---

[4] U. S. Coast Guard Historian's Office, Commandant (G-IPA-4), Washington, DC Memorandum dated September 4, 2003.

brought out storage and relighted. The hurricanes of 1915 and 1916 eroded the beach again and the tower stood six hundred feet from shore, finally, in 1918, the tower was moved 1,857 feet to its present location.[5]

About August 30,1902, Walter Andrew Roberts, Sr. transferred from the Cape Saint George Lighthouse to replace Keeper Lupton, recently transferred to the new Saint Joseph Point Rear Range Lighthouse in Port Saint Joe. Grandfather served seven years as keeper before he returned to Cape Saint George in 1909 as assistant keeper after a swapping of positions with Assistant Keeper William Knickmeyer. Grandfather told us children of the many lighthouse stories, especially the one about the three-day trips to Apalachicola for supplies, mail and food. He planted gardens, caught fish in the gulf and bay, scalloped in the bay and hunted animals, bears, raccoons and wild pigs in the woods around the cape.

On January 18, 1996, the Coast Guard discontinued the light and it exquisite 1906 Barier et Turnenne bivalve lens was covered. Hurricane Earl in September 1998 undermined one of the two turn of the century keeper's houses and left it sitting on the beach and vulnerable to the surf. About June 1999, the house was moved along with the sister house near the base of the lighthouse where they are in the process of being restored.

---

[5] 2001, <u>Florida Lighthouse Trail,</u> Thomas Taylor, Editor, (Herman Jones), Pineapple Press, Sarasota, Florida.

Roberts Family Collection

Cape San Blas Lighthouse
Keepers' Quarters
Ca 1984

Roberts Family Collection

Cape San Blas Lighthouse and Oil Storage House
CA 1984

Chapter Three

A SECOND GENERATION DEDICATION STARTS HERE
Pensacola Lighthouse, Pensacola, Florida

Roberts Family Collection

Walter Andrew Roberts, Jr.
Roberts Family Collection

My father, Walter Andrew Roberts, Jr., was born in Apalachicola, Florida, on February 29, 1896 while his father was serving as 1st Assistant Keeper at Cape St. George Lighthouse on Saint George Island.

Those around Apalachicola, Port Saint Joe, Carrabelle and the lighthouse circuits knew him as "Pete Roberts" since childhood. My mother, however, used his given name; "Walter" and I recall "Walter" being used on formal occasions and by those who didn't know him very well.

On May 30, 1916, Walter enlisted in the United States Army National Guard in Apalachicola and went overseas to France on October 6, 1916, during World War I; he served with the Medical Corps as ambulance driver and medic in France until June 25, 1919. He returned to the United States on July 6, 1919 and discharged from the army on July 15, 1919, at the Medical Base Hospital # 90, Camp Gordon, Georgia. Shortly after his army discharge, Walter Andrew Roberts, Jr., entered the United States Lighthouse Service following in his father's footsteps. Walter was assigned as 2nd Assistant Keeper at the Pensacola Lighthouse in late 1919 and he, too, trimmed his first wick at the age of 23 years as his father.

Roberts Family Collection
A Family Gathering On The Porch, Pensacola Lighthouse
Pensacola, Florida   February 1920

Son Brooks, Mrs. Thompson, wife of Keeper William D.Thompson, Miss Emma Brooks, Keeper Clem Brooks, Emma Pryor Brooks, wife of Clem Brooks, Miss Mary Ida Pryor, Keepers Shafter Johnson and Walter A. Roberts, Jr.

Roberts Family Collection
The Three Friends - Walter

Roberts Family Collection
Bessie Pryor   Ca 1917

With the beginning of World War I and after graduating from the Santa Rosa Academy in Mary Esther, Bessie Pryor went to work in Pensacola at the U. S. Post Office. Bessie was the daughter of Thomas Jefferson Pryor and Ona Rogers Pryor and great granddaughter of Jesse Rogers, members of the Pryor and Rogers founding families and developers of Pensacola and Mary Esther.

On Thanksgiving Day in 1919, she visited her cousin, Emma Pryor Brooks, whose husband, Clem, was a keeper at the lighthouse. There she met Walter Roberts, on his first assignment with the U. S. Lighthouse Service.

Walter married Bessie Pryor at the Pensacola home of a relative on October 10, 1920. After their marriage, they lived in Gulf Coast towns of Pensacola, Carrabelle, Apalachicola, and Port Saint Joe while Walter tended the lighthouses that dot the coast.

They had four children:

Walter Andrew Roberts III	b. August 3, 1921	d. February 18, 1961
William Claude Roberts	b. July 3, 1923	
Elizabeth Aileen Roberts	b. August 30, 1925	
Evelyn Janice Roberts	b. March 6, 1934	

I recall my father's story about the first Pensacola channel light was actually one-man operation in 1821. When a ship arrived at the harbor entrance after dark fired a cannon, the light attendant on shore would raise a light to the top of a flagstaff. The incoming captain would use the light as a guide to steer his ship into the harbor. This was not a permanent solution to the problem and territorial senators worked to find a solution to the eternal problem. They located an inactive lightship, Aurora Borealis, at the mouth of the Mississippi River, where it was no longer needed and arranged to have the ship transferred to Pensacola Bay. The Aurora Borealis arrived on site about June 1823 and anchored east of the channel entrance. The lightship did not solve the problem, the bad weather problem was a recurring one and the vessel lost an anchor on more than one occasion. In an effort to protect the lightship from the onslaught of the Gulf of Mexico, the ship was moved behind a barrier island to the east and off the channel. This move made the vessel more useless as an aid to navigation.

In early 1823, Congress appropriated some $ 6,000 for a lighthouse near Pensacola Bay. The site chosen was on a bluff, just west of Fort Barrancas. Within a short time, construction was completed and on December 20, 1824, a light brightened the Pensacola Bay sky at the south entrance to Pensacola Bay, making the light 60 feet above sea level and lighted it in 1825, making it the first lighthouse built by the government on Florida's Gulf Coast. A new round, white brick tower stood about thirty feet tall and near the tower were the keeper's quarters, a small one story brick building with an attached kitchen with a well and outhouse nearby. The lighthouse station fell into disfavor with shippers as being inadequate navigational aids. This caused several problems with the recently established U. S. Navy's shipyard since many of its ships were of the largest class and required more nighttime navigation assistance. Another problem arose after an inspection report noted that the Pensacola light could not be seen a good distance due to many wrongly installed panes of glass and the light was being obscured by trees along the coastline. The light with reflectors went out of date. A recent archeological excavation located where the building and tower once stood. The site of the first tower is about midway between Fort Barrancas and the present lighthouse to the west. In 1856, engineers began construction of a new tower on the north side of the bay entrance. The tower stands 171 feet from ground to focal plane and 191 feet from sea level to focal plane. Lighted on January 1, 1859, the first order revolving light gave to the harbor the necessary beacon. In 1869, a first order lens replaced a fourth order lens installed in 1863. The still operating light is a First Order Fresnel Lens. The lens has 344 prisms set in a beehive design. The lighthouse has two 1,000-watt bulbs in the light (a primary and a back up) controlled by light sensor switches. The lens magnifies the light to 40,000 candlepower and appears to flash at 20-second intervals and can be seen for 27 miles. Prior to the installation of electricity in 1939, the keepers pulled chains weights of the clockwork mechanism every two hours to keep the lens rotating. Every evening, a keeper climbed the 177 steps to the lantern room with a five gallon, 40 pound can of oil for the lantern's nightly chore.

In 1921, Walter transferred to the Crooked River Lighthouse in Carrabelle, Florida, as 1st Assistant Keeper.

The tower was originally painted white but today the lower third is painted white and upper two thirds is painted black. The lighthouse is located on the Pensacola Naval Air Station on State Route 295 South.

Undated Photo US Coast Guard Files

Front Range Light

Chapter Four

Crooked River Lighthouse, Carrabelle, Florida

Roberts Family Collection

In 1838, workers built a lighthouse on the west end of Dog Island, off Carrabelle, installed a revolving light to distinguish it from the Cape St. George Lighthouse to the southeast. In 1872, storms pushed the tower one foot out of perpendicular, which necessitated the removal of the lens to the top of the keeper's dwelling. A hurricane in 1873 toppled both the tower and the keeper's dwelling into the bay. In 1889, Congress authorized $40,000 to build a lighthouse in Carrabelle, to replace the one on Dog Island, but construction was postponed until 1894-1895. Work on the structure was finished in August 1895 and a fourth order lens 115 feet above sea level began operating on October 18, 1895. Two identical keepers' dwellings, a washhouse, oil storage building and tool shed were built adjoining the lighthouse. The keepers' dwellings have been dismantled and removed leaving the tower standing alone.

The Crooked River, which gave its name to the new lighthouse, empties into the Ochlocknee River to the east and the Carrabelle River to the west. Eda Pickett Kilbourn, a long ago Carrabelle resident, once composed a musical etude about her hometown. An exercise for the pianoforte, it was called "The Ripples of Carrabelle" and orchestrated the flow of the Carrabelle River as it moved past town into the Gulf of Mexico. No one remembers or plays the lyric melody today but it could well describe life in the close-to-last of Florida's Gulf Coast fishing villages. Carrabelle is an island unto itself, located on the Isle of Saint James and bounded by the New River to the west, the Ochlockonee River to the east, the Crooked River to the north and the Gulf of Mexico to the south. Carrabelle's beginnings are both obscure and subject for debate among history buffs. A Spanish explorer, Pamilio de Narvez, is known to have chartered the area in the early 1700s. One group holds it was he who named the river, Rio Carrabelle, "beautiful river" in his native language.

There are some dim records of trappers and hunters camping at the mouth of the Carrabelle River about 1850; these camps are believed to have been the beginning of the first settlements. In 1878, the U. S. Post Office registered the town as "Rio Carrabelle" so the town of Carrabelle did exist. The "Rio" was dropped officially within three years. [6]

Mrs. Ida Ethel Kilbourn Brown, granddaughter of pioneer settlers, James Pickett and Frances Yent Pickett, recalled with fondness the picnics and socials at the Crooked River Lighthouse. A beacon since 1895 and in more serene times, the ladies would spread elaborate lunches at the tower base for their Sunday beaux.

---

[6] Ann Frances Dolan, (ca 1982), "Carrabelle Florida", The Southern Magazine

James Albert William was named the first keeper in 1895 and served until 1906 at an annual salary of $600 and Tip Warren was the first Assistant Keeper and he served until 1896 at an annual salary of $450.

Walter Andrew Roberts, Jr., transferred to Crooked River Lighthouse, Carrabelle, Florida in 1921. He served as 1st Assistant Keeper from 1921 until 1925 under Keeper Thornwald Hansen. Keeper Hansen had replaced the retired keeper prior to Dad's arrival on station.

My brother, Walter Andrew Roberts III, was born on August 3, 1921, at Grandfather Roberts' house in Apalachicola while Dad was the assistant keeper at Crooked River Lighthouse. My parents traveled by boat from the light station to Apalachicola, as there were no roads; the boat was their only contact with the outside world.

In July 1923, their second son, William, was born and I have always told my family and friends that I was born at the lighthouse; I really believed it to be true until I probated my parents' estate in 1979. During the probate proceedings, I found my baby book in Mother's hope chest; the notes and pictures indicated that I was born at the Carrabelle home of Mrs. Frances Pickett.[7] Mrs. Frances Pickett & Doctor A. E. Russell was attending nurse and physician. Carrabelle's senior citizens, James Reynolds Pickett and Frances Josephine Yent Pickett settled in Carrabelle in 1892.

In January 2002, I addressed the St. Joseph Historical Society in Port Saint Joe and met Mrs. Pickett's great granddaughter, Elizabeth Brown Stokoe. The following week, Elizabeth sent Pickett family photographs and articles about Carrabelle of long ago and several months later at a television show taping, I met Boyd Pickett, Mrs. Pickett's great grandson. What a pleasure to meet Mrs. Pickett's descendants and to receive those treasures of history and to relive my birthplace. It's a small world after all and such a joy to receive those wonderful gifts from her great-grandchildren.

---

[7] Baby Days, 1924, William C. Roberts.

Roberts Family Collection

Picture Taken In 1894 Shows Station Under Construciton

Lighthouse Lens Inventory
Crooked River Light Station Lens

Fourth-order bivalve (1/3 open) Fresnel lens made by Henry Lepaute in 1894 is on display U.S. Coast Guard 8th District Offices in New Orleans, Louisiana. May be viewed by prior appointment. Photo by BMC Larry Davis,USCG

Florida State Archives

Crooked River Lighthouse
Carrabelle, Florida
Ca 1966

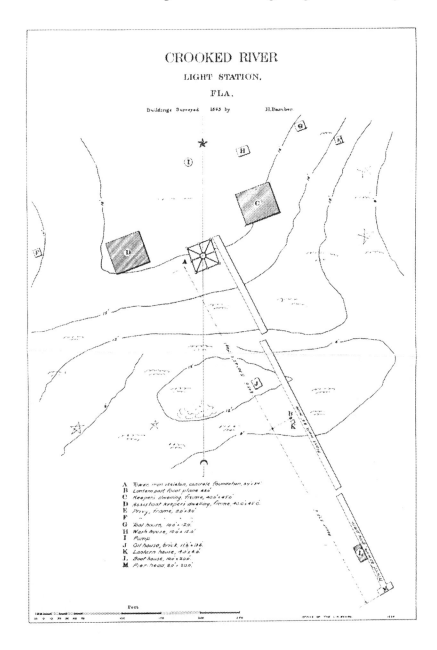

Crooked River Lighthouse, Carrabelle, Florida
Survey Plot Plan 1893
Surveyor: H. Bamber

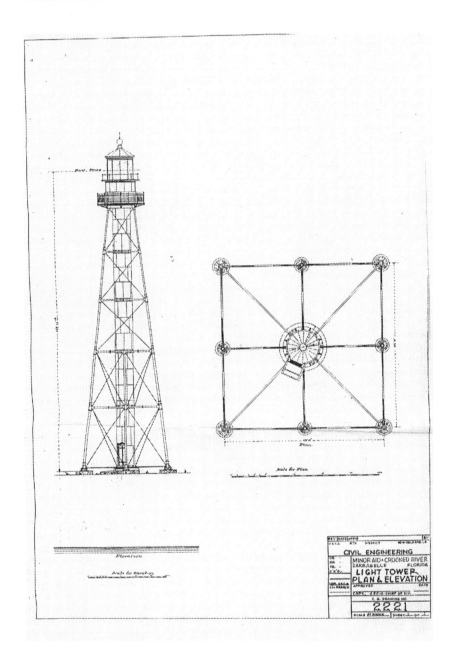

Crooked River Lighthouse, Carrabelle, Florida
Light Tower Plan & Elevation

R. Topping Photo
Carrabelle Harbor

Carrabelle's Consolidated School in the late 1930's. The building, which housed grades 1 through 12, has been replaced by separate high and grade schools.

1843 – 1912 *and in memory of:* 1849 – 1936

James Reynolds Pickett, and Frances Josephine Yent Pickett

Mrs. Ida Ethel Kilbourn Browne displays a painting she made of the Crooked River Lighthouse. Note caretaker's cottages on either side. Holding the painting's other side is her grandson, Christopher Wells. (Photo by Dell Fadio)

Chapter Five

Cape Saint George Lighthouse, Apalachicola, Florida

Roberts Family Collection

Walter Roberts Comes Home!

The Cape Saint George Lighthouse, located on Little Saint George Island, blinked on in 1833. The tower rose 65 feet and held 13 lamps intensified by reflectors. In 1847, a new lighthouse was built two miles from the original site. It lasted four years before being toppled by a storm. The third lighthouse, 72 feet high was built in 1852, although damaged during the Civil War and washed by many storms, still stands today.

In 1925, Walter Andrew Roberts, Jr. transferred to Cape St. George Lighthouse, Apalachicola, Florida, as 1st Assistant Keeper and reported to Keeper David D. Silva, Sr. We moved into the assistant keeper's quarters, the same house he had lived in as a child when his father was assistant keeper under Keeper Porter. He had come home! We lived in the assistant's house for a few years and I have wonderful memories of our family and life there. My sister, Elizabeth (Betty) was born in Apalachicola during our first years at Cape St. George Lighthouse.

During our early years on the island, Keeper Silva's grand children, Connelly, Henry and Jamie Raiford, often spent the summers on the island so we children had playmates to help pass the hours. We looked forward to seeing them each summer; exploring the island, swimming, playing games and just having a good time. Keeper Silva's son, David and his family lived in a cottage on the bay side of the island but his two children, David Cleveland and Dorothy, were much younger than us; we knew them but not as playmates.

Later, my parents bought a home in Apalachicola so the children could go to school. At that time, Walter was the only child old enough to attend school. The large house on 12th Street had four bedrooms; living room; a long hall extended from the front entry to the large dining area, bedrooms were on each side of the hall and porches around the house gave the house a massive look.

My parents were generous in many ways; three acts of generosity come to mind; they invited three family friends to share our home during the 1920 depression years. Mrs. Elizabeth Montgomery Lewis recalls about 1926; her family lived in our house until her father, Asa Montgomery, located a home for the family on 17th Street. She recalls that my sister, Betty, and I were very young and my brother, Walter, was almost school age. In later years I attended Port Saint Joe High School with Elizabeth's brother, Billy and worked as a clerk at the Quality Grocery; Mr. Montgomery managed the market. About 1928, the second family to share our home was mother's cousin, Emma Brooks and her new husband, Richard (Bunks) Porter. Emma and Bunks lived there for several years, in 1930, their first daughter, Emma Jo, was born at our house on 12th Street. The Porter children later recalled having fun at the big house, being chased by the boys, playing tag, other games and running around the porches. The Paul Farmer family lived with us for several years until Paul could find adequate housing for his wife, and son, Paul James. Paul James and I became great friends and were constant companions in all our doings.

When I was four years old, my parents agreed I could spend the next two years on Saint George Island with my father until I was school age. As Dad and I took care of the lighthouse on the island, Mother took care of her two children in Apalachicola; they spent the summers and holidays on the island with us.

Dad taught me how to fish, bait a hook, steer the lighthouse boat, steer the horse and wagon and to navigate the deep waters of Apalachicola Bay using the beacons and buoys. I learned how to read a compass before I went to school. He taught me the meaning of doing a job right the first time, responsibilities, honesty and loyalty.

He let me steer the boat on the days we "tended" the beacons in the bay. The five or six beacons burned kerosene and we refueled the beacons on a set schedule. On days when the bay was calm, I would steer the boat to a beacon ladder; Dad would stand on the bow of the boat with a five-gallon kerosene can in the crook of his elbow; climb the ladder; refuel the beacon as I circled the boat around the beacon until he signaled. I drove the boat to the ladder, he would get on board and we would be off to the next beacon. On days when the bay was rough or rainy, I became the designated rider as Keeper Silva and Dad took care of the steering.

I often steered the boat on our weekly trips to Apalachicola for supplies and mail. We always docked the lighthouse boat at the Marks Brokerage Company docks on the Apalachicola River waterfront and visited with Dad's friends, DeWitt, Homer and Aubrey Marks while we shopped for groceries. During the summer, Dad kept our car parked in a garage near the Marks Brokerage Company building. When we completed our shopping and errand running, we stopped by the Jitney Jungle store for a few slices of sandwich meat (called "boneless ham"), bread, mayonnaise and soft drinks (Cokes were known as "dopes") and drove to our house for lunch. Our friends, the Porters, nicknamed me "Cap'n" and called me by that name until I was a teenager and moved to Port Saint Joe.

One of my jobs was to help Dad with painting chores around the station, working on lights and boat repairs. I remember one cold day he was working in the boat on the lift and asked for a wrench (I was in charge of the toolbox), I handed the wrench to him but it slipped out of my hand and fell into the water. Being four or five years old, I became frightened as to what he might say or do. Without hesitation, he removed his clothes and jumped into the water, dove to the bottom and picked up the wrench. I thought he was Superman! While drying and putting on his clothes, he looked at me, smiled and said "No big deal". Those may not be his exact words but that is the kind of person he was.

One of my daily tasks was to assist Dad with preparing the lantern room each morning after the light was extinguished. He would wipe, clean and polish the lens and brass works while I hung the canvas curtains using a long pole with a gadget on the end to hold the curtain rings. The curtains were hung on three sides of the lantern room to keep the sun off the lens. The curtains were made of soft canvas material about three feet wide and six feet long and hung from the wall hooks. The curtains were taken down at sundown, folded and neatly stowed in the lantern room until the next morning when they were hung for the day. We did not use curtains on the north side of the lantern room.

Dad was appointed Keeper about 1930 and Mr. Thornton K. Cooper ("Gus") was appointed Assistant Keeper. Keeper Cooper was a bachelor and took the Roberts children under his wing to teach us, rear us and be an uncle to us. We moved into the keeper's big house. What an improvement in space and living area; a porch all around, connecting kitchen, large fireplaces in all of the rooms, water in the kitchen (hand pumped from the water cistern outside). My second sister, Evelyn (Jan) was born in Apalachicola on March 6, 1934; now our family was complete.

During the years of the late 1920s and 1930s we children had to entertain ourselves every day with the help of our parents, as there was no other family living on Saint George Island during our growing up period. Growing up during the depression years was good discipline; a lot of things were taken for granted today didn't exist then.

There were no roads, automobiles, TV, running water nor any other convenience except a telephone line to Apalachicola for safety and emergency uses installed at the insistence of the Lighthouse Service. Our only transportation was horse and wagon. The station's water supply was kept in three cisterns; rainwater was captured using gutters and downspouts on the two houses.

My family entertained us with special outings, fish fries and games; on days a fish fry was scheduled, Dad and I would load the wagon with cast nets, old shoes, hats and buckets. My brother would drive us in the wagon to the Gap, a wide level spot; about two-three miles from the lighthouse toward Big Saint George. He would deposit us and return to the lighthouse to collect the fish fry goodies, Mother and Betty while Dad and I were catching the fish, usually mullet in the shallow waters around the Gap. When we had enough fish, we cleaned the fish, gathered wood and old bricks to make a fire rack to hold a blackened iron Dutch oven to fry the fish. When Mother, Betty and Walter arrived, we were ready to start the family fun. We always had plenty of fish, fries and all the goodies Mother brought. After dinner, we played games and told stories. What exciting times we had!

My Mother staged the most popular of all the games we played at the lighthouse called "Hocus Pocus". She would arrange for each child to enter a dark stand up closet containing a large hamper covered with a clean white sheet. The person would stand in front of the hamper waving his hands like a magician over the hamper while saying the words *"hocus pocus, diamond ocus"* three times. The magician would remove the white sheet to discover a nice surprise, usually an apple, orange, candy or a small gift. Mother arranged the game so that every child got a different gift. I remember in one game all three of us found white painter caps under the sheet and we wore those caps every day.

The game was so popular with all of our young guests; they wanted to play often. My grown-up cousins still talk about "hocus pocus" every time we meet.

Our family friend, Neil Hinkley, owned a Shetland pony named "Prince". Around 1930, Prince became a problem for the Hinkleys to board and keep so Neil's mother asked Dad to take Prince to St. George Island and she made arrangements to have Prince moved to the island on a friend's fish boat.

It was decided that Prince should pull a wagon to ride the children. Dad bought a bright fire engine red unassembled wagon from the Montgomery Ward catalogue. As Mr. Cooper and Dad assembled the wagon, Mother designed and made a harness for the pony. This was a thing of beauty but alas, we could not get Prince in position to put on the harness and so we could not hitch Prince to the wagon. No way was he going to pull the wagon. What could we do with a brand new red wagon?

Dad suggested we could get a goat from Sand Island to pull the wagon. (Sand Island is the western tip of Little St. George Island about 2-3 miles from the lighthouse). We laughed and said we thought that was the funniest thing we had ever heard, a goat wagon? Well, the next day, Dad and I rode our horses to Sand Island to find a goat. We took Trixie to help us; Dad told Trixie to find us a goat, well, she did. Trixie ran through the herd of wild goats and stopped beside a beautiful male goat with long curved horns. The goat did not move as Trixie stood beside him; Dad rode up to the goat puts a rope around his horns and started for the lighthouse

The goat did not offer any resistance and followed us home. We fed, petted and watered the goat for several days while Mother remodeled the pony harness to fit the goat. Of course, we named the goat "Billy".

In a few days, we decided to test Billy with the wagon. That was the easiest thing we ever did. Billy acted as if he had always pulled a wagon. We did not use pony bits in his mouth but we used a rope around his nose to control him. Dad used the rope to lead Billy pulling the wagon with three children riding in the wagon. Later, it was not necessary for Dad to lead Billy; he seemed to enjoy his new job; my brother would hitch Billy to the wagon and we were off on another ride nearly every afternoon!

When our summer vacation was almost over, Dad and I would take Billy back to Sand Island to be with his friends for the winter months. At the start of next year's vacation, we rode to Sand Island and Trixie found Billy in the herd and went to him. Again, Dad put the rope around Billy's horns and led him back to the lighthouse for another summer of fun. We did this same thing each summer and had four summers of fun with Billy and the red wagon. Some of you may find this yarn had to believe but those of us that lived it know it to be true.

Roberts Family Collection

William & The Goat Cart
Ca 1930

Roberts Family Collection

William Walter & Prince Ca 1930

Roberts Family Collection
William & Walter Riding Ole Neb
Ca 1930

Roberts Family Collection

An Afternoon Outing
The Roberts Children of Cape St. George
Ca 1930
Note the white painter caps

Roberts Family Collection

Trixie, Alice and Friends
Trixie   Walter   Alice   Elizabeth   William
Ca 1930

U. S. Coast Guard Photo   Ca 1940
The Cape Saint George Lighthouse, Apalachicola, Florida

On one of our afternoon rides we found a black and white spotted piglet in one of our caves. Our "caves" were scrub oak trees overgrown and bowed over to present a cave-like appearance. We searched the area for her mother but we could not find her so we took the piglet home, adopted her and named her "Alice" after a friend in Apalachicola. I am sure that Alice in Apalachicola did not know we used her name for our pig. Alice and Trixie followed closely behind the children all summer waiting for the next escapade, to be fed or petted. Our Alice stayed with us all that summer and Dad cared for her during the winter months. One summer, Alice came home with a litter of her own little ones; we appropriately named every one for members of Apalachicola Alice's family.

One afternoon, my brother, Walter, and I decided to go camping in one of our caves not too far from the lighthouse. We took Trixie and Alice to the cave for company. We had our camping gear, food, water, bedrolls and all the stuff necessary to camp. After tiring from playing with Alice and Trixie, walking on the beach and eating supper, we retired for the night. After a long time, Walter got up, built a campfire and began to prepare breakfast. I thought it was too early but he said the sun was coming up and he was hungry. As we were eating, we heard Trixie barking and noises on the beach. Our Dad rode up to our cave and told us that Mother was worried about us and wanted us to come home. Walter told Dad we hadn't finished breakfast; Dad told us to finish breakfast and come on home, as Mother was concerned about us. We packed up and went home, the clock on the mantel told us it was 10:00 P. M.

The Lighthouse Service had rigid visitor procedures at their lighthouses. Daytime visitors were allowed on site until sundown and overnight visitors were permitted only if authorized in advance by the District Commissioner's written passes (called "permits") not to exceed two weeks. To obtain a permit for our friends to visit, Dad requested a permit be issued to the visitor, far in advance of the visit and outlined name, age, days of visit and reason for visit. Our annual summer visitor for many years was our young family friend, Rodman Porter, Jr., of Apalachicola. Rodman was always ready to visit when school was out and the Roberts family moved to Cape Saint George for the summer. Rodman spent many summers with us doing the childhood things that we enjoyed. He always brought special toys, gadgets and new things to try out; one year we had "Buck Rogers" laser guns that made loud popping sounds. These sounds frightened the horses so Dad would not permit us to use the guns when the horses were close by. One summer, we tried a water pump on the beach; we actually got fresh drinking water along the edge of the gulf. My parents erected two camping tents near the lighthouse for us to camp out; we had cots, chairs and tables and often slept in the tents. I recall and smile at the wonderful days and times spent by Walter, Betty, Rodman and me as the Children of Cape Saint George.

Walter and I had miniature sail boats (made by our father), rigged to sail in a large pond on the beach. We set the rudders to permit the boat to sail to the other side of the pond; we'd race around and reset the rudders for a return visit. I still have my sailboat; she's dry docked needing repairs and a new sail.

The Sea Queen is still alive after all these years! Later, Dad and Mr. Cooper built us a real sailboat. It was a beautiful ship, red sails, centerboard, tiller and rudder. We kept the boat on the bay side of the island at the lighthouse pier and boat. The bay was much better for sailing a small boat than the rough gulf. We sailed the boat often while waiting for Dad to return from town.

Another one of our tasks was to hitch the horse and wagon to take Dad to the boat and pier on the bay side on days he went to Apalachicola. He always telephoned to tell us he was leaving town and approximate time he would be at the lighthouse pier. Some of those days, Walter and I would leave the lighthouse a little early to do some fishing, crabbing or sailing in our new boat. We had wonderful times together.

I mentioned earlier the Lighthouse Service required keepers to record the air and water temperatures twice daily. The past keeper performed this task after his grandchildren collected the seawater; then they would yell to their grandfather "Temperature"; he would stop his work and record the temperatures. My Mother thought this was unnecessary.

When Dad became keeper and assumed this task, Mother taught Walter and me to read a thermometer and we recorded the temperatures after that lesson. No more yelling "Temperature". During the winter holidays, Mother designed a system to collect seawater without getting barefooted or getting wet. She designed a reel & rod like gismo on a long pole to dip the bucket in the gulf thus keeping our clothes and feet dry. Of course, we did not use this gismo during the summer, too much fun getting wet!

Everything at the station had to be kept spic and span. We children helped to keep it clean as part of our being there. A Lighthouse Service Inspector checked the station quarterly and we always knew when he was coming as Dad had to meet him in Apalachicola and bring him to the station on the lighthouse boat. No surprise visits at this station. That extra hour or so gave Mr. Cooper and us a bonus to find and clean any missed areas. The inspector checked the records of daily activities and the items listed in the directive to determine if the keepers were properly performing their duties and the manner in which they performed. When the inspector (usually Mr. Lamphier) completed his thorough inspection and made his written reports, Mother always prepared a big Apalachicola seafood dinner for him, his favorite oysters, crabs, fish and shrimp. Mr. Lamphier was our favorite inspector and usually brought us children candies and a small toy. I think he was Dad's favorite, too, as they had mutual respect and admiration for each other's professionalism, devotion to duty and the Lighthouse Service. Some years later, I learned that Mr. Lamphier was actually Mr. E. S. Lamphier, Superintendent of Lighthouses! The rewards for an efficient lighthouse station was the District Inspector's Efficiency Pin (Red); awarded to the keeper whose station was the most efficient in its district for one year and the Commissioner's Efficiency Pin (Blue) was awarded to the keeper whose station was the most efficient in its district for three straight years. My father earned several of these pins during his long career.

Dad served as keeper at Cape St. George Lighthouse until June 30, 1938 when he was assigned to the Beacon Hill Lighthouse in Port Saint Joe, Florida.

Florida State Archives
Refueling A Kerosene Lighted Beacon in Apalachicola Bay

Roberts Family Collection

Cape Saint George Lighthouse, Apalachicola, Florida
Left: Bessie Roberts, Wife of Assistant Keeper Pete Roberts
Center: Malveena Silva, Daughter-in-law of Keeper David Silva
Right: Keeper David Silva, Sr.   Ca 1925

Roberts Family Collection

Cape Saint George Lighthouse, Apalachicola, Florida
Painting the Lighthouse Tower
Ca 1930

Roberts Family Collection

Cape Saint George Lighthouse
Bayside Boat House and Pier
Ca 1925

Chapter Six

Saint Joseph Point Rear Range Light Station
Port Saint Joe, Florida

Roberts Family Collection

Since the early 1800s, lighthouses were important landmarks along the Florida Gulf Coast. St. Joseph Bay had two lighthouses during this period. One, known as the St. Joseph Bay Lighthouse, stood at the tip of the long peninsular that encircles the bay. The Cape San Blas Lighthouse, the other beacon, was located at the crook of this curving narrow strip of land.

The St. Joseph Bay Lighthouse on the tip of the peninsular was completed on February 23, 1839 and the fourteen lamps of its light were lighted shortly thereafter. In 1843, the Collector of Customs declared the St.

Joseph Bay Lighthouse was in poor condition and a decision was made to abandon the lighthouse. In 1846, the government issued a contract to build a new Cape San Blas Lighthouse to the south. In 1901, the Lighthouse Service decided to build a new lighthouse on the mainland and in 1902; a new lighthouse was built at Beacon Hill, ten miles west of Port Saint Joe. It was officially named the St. Joseph Point Rear Range Light but locally known as the Beacon Hill Lighthouse. Workers finished the building and a six-foot wide 245-foot long pier in 1902. [8]

The building was raised 10-12 feet off the ground on brick pillars. The keeper's house consisted of three bedrooms, living room and kitchen/dining room. There were shiny white railings and gray painted porch decks on three sides of the house. On top of the house was the lantern room housing a third order Fresnel lens that showed a fixed white light 90 feet above sea level; the light could be seen 13 miles at sea. This was one of a few lighthouses that the Lighthouse Service permitted the keeper's family to reside in the lighthouse; other stations provided family quarters near the lighthouse.

The Front Range Light stood near the beach about 600 feet from the lighthouse down a narrow red brick walkway. The beacon's original small lantern was lowered to ground level, filled with kerosene and the lantern lighted by the keeper and raised to the top of the tripod or lantern support by mean of a block and tackle. In 1936, an electric flasher unit changed the fixed white light to a four-second white flash followed by a six-second eclipse. The Front Range lantern was electrified at the same time the Rear Range lighthouse lantern characteristic change was made.

The newly appointed keeper, Charles Lupton, lit the lantern on August 1, 1902. Mr. Lupton was formerly keeper at the Cape San Blas Lighthouse. He hired Ms. Lillian McNeill; a teacher from Money Bayou, to come stay at the lighthouse so his children could get an

---

[8] U. S. Coast Guard Historian's Office, Commandant, (G-IPA-4), Washington, DC Memorandum dated September 4, 2003.

education. She taught the children for several years for $15 a month plus room and board.

Walter Andrew Roberts, Jr. arrived at the St. Joseph Point Rear Range Light Station on June 30, 1938, to relieve retiring Keeper Thomas Clarman (Clem) Brooks. Dad was to be the third and last keeper of this Gulf Coast station. Keeper Charles Lupton had served for 26 years when he retired in 1928 then came Keeper Clem Brooks for ten years; followed by Keeper Walter Roberts in 1938.

This lighthouse had all modern conveniences, e.g., running water, electricity, bathroom, telephone and an icebox. The iceman, Mr. Bo Brown, came nearly every day to service the icebox and Mother had a pot of coffee ready for he and Dad. Mr. Brown and Dad's friendship began in Apalachicola many years before when Mr. Brown was Service Manager for the Otto Anderson Ford Company when Dad bought Mother a 1925-26 Model T Ford. In 1936, Dad bought a new Ford and Mr. Otto parked the 1925 Model T in the middle of Main Street in front of the Grill Café so everybody would know that Dad had traded cars and they could see the excellent condition of the Model T.

This assignment to the Beacon Hill Lighthouse was indeed a plum for our Dad. We were only ten miles from town on a paved highway. The only beacon was near the highway at the end of a 600-foot brick walkway; Dad did not have to "tend" beacons in the bay or gulf. I never felt I was living on a lighthouse station here. This lighthouse did not have a boat, beacons or a pier on the beach. The paved highway was too close to the lighthouse to be a remote and romantic lighthouse site.

In 1939, the United States Coast Guard assumed command of all lighthouses, beacons and aids to navigation. Dad had three options, one option was to retire; remain as a civilian and the third option was enlistment in the Coast Guard. He opted for enlistment in the Coast Guard as Chief Petty Officer and served for 13 years.

Dad said, "This assignment was the nicest I ever had. It's only 10 miles out of Port Saint Joe. The lighthouse home with a flashing light built on top of the house we lived in and the light was reached through steps in the living room".

When the Coast Guard informed Dad that a photographer was coming to take the official picture of the lighthouse, Dad set tasks for all of us to do; rake yards, pick up trash, paint fences, etc. The station had to be spic and span per Dad's usual procedures for the picture taking. All tasks were completed and the official picture was made, lo and behold, someone forgot to close a gate!

Of course, Dad assigned tasks here, too. I remember one of my daily tasks was empting the icebox drain tray. It was fun for a while, it got me off other tasks, but it became a chore, empting the drain tray into a bucket and taking it down the long flight of stairs. Sometimes, I would forget to do this and the water would flood the pantry floor. My job then was to mop and clean the pantry floor. There just had to be a better way. One day, I had a brilliant idea – what if I put a hole in the floor, insert a hose in the drain tray and push the hose through the hole in the floor thus allowing the water to drain outside? I thought this to be an excellent idea, so I did it. All went well until Dad saw the water dripping under the house and called for an investigation. He finally approved my icebox drain system and the icebox drained automatically for years!

During World War II, during the evening hours many ships plying the Gulf of Mexico anchored for safety in the deep waters of St. Joseph Bay. During the early war years, two young Coast Guardsmen were assigned to the station, living with the keeper's family. Their main duties were lookouts and general station maintenance. Later during the war, about 1943, the ground floor of the lighthouse was enclosed to make living quarters for the contingent of Coast Guardsmen assigned to the station. Their duties were to act as lookouts from the tower to detect activities in the gulf, patrol the beaches on horseback and guard against spies coming ashore from German submarines that were known to prowl the Gulf of Mexico. The horses were stabled on a plot of land several hundred yards east of the lighthouse behind the sand dunes along the highway. The government erected a stable, a barn and horse pens to house the horses and equipment.

By the 1950s, the majority of the keepers were military and many of the traditions of lighthouse keeping were lost. This greatly reduced the continuity and much care of lighthouse equipment, particularly lenses were lost and by the mid 1950s, all lighthouse stations, save the Boston Harbor Lighthouse, were automated.

Walter retired from the Coast Guard when the station deactivated in 1952. He remained on station for approximately 10 months as a civilian custodian pending disposal of government equipment and property. In 1953, following his retirement from the Coast Guard, Walter and Bessie moved to Mary Esther, Florida.

Following retirement in 1952, Walter worked eight years for an electronics company at Eglin Air Force Base, Florida, and retired for a second time. Later, he worked at the Mary Esther Post Office for fourteen years, again following in the footsteps of his father.

Walter Andrew Roberts, Jr. died in the West Florida Medical Center, Pensacola, Florida, on October 3, 1977, and was buried in Jesse Rogers Cemetery, Mary Esther, Florida. Bessie Pryor Roberts died in Fort Walton Beach, Florida, on February 7, 1978, and was buried beside Walter in the Jesse Rogers Cemetery, Mary Esther.

The Front Range Light, which was located seaward of the Beacon Hill Lighthouse for over fifty years, found its way home in October 2001. On a Thursday, early in October 2001, U. S. Coast Guard officials hand delivered the range light to members of the Saint Joseph Historical Society during a brief ceremony at the Gulf Coast Library. The light was commissioned in 1902; decommissioned and removed from its location at Beacon Hill about 1960. The light will remain on display in the library as a historical marker.

In January 2002, I offered my help to locate and obtain the lighthouse's third order lens for Society's display room. First, what we were looking for was a fixed third order Fresnel lens. A 1927 inventory record shows the third order lens for the St. Joseph Point Rear Range Light was manufactured by Phares & Fanaux (Barbier, Bernard & Trienes) but the inventory does not list a date of manufacture or serial number, so probably the serial number was not stamped on the lens. In fact, that lens is the only one in Florida by that manufacturer. The Society contacted the local Aids to Navigation Team in the Northwest Florida area but the Team could provide no information as to the whereabouts of the lens. When I checked with the U. S. Coast Guard Washington Office, (Public Affairs Staff, COMDT (G-IPA-4), the Curator, Gail Fuller, wrote she had checked all her resources but found no information on the current location of the third order lens but promised to keep the file open and the search will continue.

Roberts Family Collection
The Front Range Light

Roberts Family Collection
The Famous 600 foot Red Brick Walk
Ca 1938

Roberts Family Collection
Walter Andrew Roberts, Jr.
Wife, Bessie & Daughter, Janice
Early 1940s

Roberts Family Collection

Ca 1940   Ca 1950

Walter Andrew Roberts, Jr.
Chief Petty Officer
U. S. Coast Guard

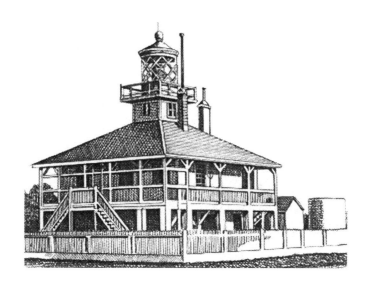

The Beacon Hill Lighthouse
Pencil Sketch By Paul Bradley

David Maddox Family Collection

St. Joseph Point Rear Range Lighthouse
Port Saint Joe, Florida   Ca. 1943

Note the horse barn/stables and corral (white square) behind the sand dunes along the highway several hundred yards to the right of the lighthouse

U.S. Coast Guard Archives
Ca. 1950

U. S. Coast Guard Archives
Ca. 1915

Chapter Seven

A THIRD GENERATION DEDICATION STARTS HERE...
Crooked River Lighthouse, Carrabelle, Florida

Roberts Family Collection
Crooked River Lighthouse

Roberts Family Collection
Walter Andrew Roberts III

Another Walter Roberts Comes Home!

Walter Andrew Roberts III was born in Apalachicola in 1921. He lived at this lighthouse while his father was 1st Assistant Keeper at the Crooked River Lighthouse and enlisted in the U. S. Coast Guard in New Orleans in 1941. After basic training, he received an assignment to the Crooked River Lighthouse in Carrabelle and served on station for about four years. He had come home, too, following in the footsteps of his father. The 1,600 or so population is a mix of oldsters who remember a serene, turn-of-the-century Carrabelle, and the middle-aged who came during World War II, when it teemed with servicemen from nearby military encampments and enjoyed a boom. Some young men stayed on to fish or take over family businesses.[9]

On 27 October 1946, he married Madeline Soderberg of Port St. Joe, Florida, and they had one son, Walter Arthur Roberts, born in Jacksonville, Florida, on February 11, 1948. Walter received a medical discharge from the Coast Guard and died in Jacksonville on February 18, 1961. Walter was buried in the Jesse Rogers Cemetery, Mary Esther, Florida. Madeline Soderberg Roberts died in July 1998 and was buried beside Walter in Jesse Rogers Cemetery, Mary Esther, Florida.

---

[9] Ann Frances Dolan (ca 1982), "Carrabelle, Florida", The Southern Magazine, Page 12

John Canetta Collection

Crooked River Lighthouse, Carrabelle, Florida
Ca. 2004

Roberts Family Collection

Walter Andrew Roberts III
Ca 1943

Chapter Eight

The Dog Island Lighthouse
Carrabelle, Florida

A skeleton tower that now sits outside the town of Carrabelle replaced a lighthouse on Dog Island off the coast. In 1838, workers built a lighthouse on the west end of Dog Island, off Carrabelle, Florida, installed a revolving light to distinguish it from the Cape Saint George Lighthouse to the southwest. This Dog Island light was to guard the entrance to the Saint George Sound in the east entrance to the Gulf of Mexico. Dog Island may have gotten its name from wild dogs on the island when the French explored the area in the 1500s. The seven-mile long, 2,000-acre island once housed a federal government facility that included a lighthouse and quarantine station for ship entering the port. The exposed nature of the site led to many damages from gales in the 1840s and from fires set during the Civil War by Confederates who wished to prevent federal troops from using the tower as a lookout post.

The Dog Island Lighthouse is directly responsible for the existence of the Crooked River Lighthouse. It was only a matter of months after the completion of the original Cape Saint George Lighthouse, which local citizens of Apalachicola began to see a need for a lighthouse on Dog Island. The reason was presented to Congress that Apalachicola continued to grow and larger ships were calling at the port city from far away as Europe. The large ships could not navigate the West Pass because of sand bar in the area. But as they shrewdly pointed out, at the East Pass there was already a channel that, if properly lighted and marked with buoys, would allow large ships to enter and then continue through the Saint George Sound into Apalachicola Bay and into the port city.

Finally, in early 1837, Congress approved the sum of $11,000 for lighthouse and buoys in East Pass. The lighthouse was only two years old when the first deterioration problems began. This was followed by a hurricane in the fall of 1842, which blew down about one half of the lighthouse and swept away the keeper's house.

A second lighthouse was erected the following spring but the hurricane of 1851 destroyed three other lighthouses including Dog Island. The lighthouse was rebuilt in 1852 only to be destroyed by another hurricane. Late in 1872, several storms had pushed the tower one foot out of perpendicular, which necessitated the removal of the lens to the top of the keeper's dwelling. A hurricane in 1873 toppled both the tower and keeper's quarters into the bay. Congress appropriated approximately $20,000 to rebuild the tower but the money was never spent and the Lighthouse Board decided that local commerce was not developing enough to warrant a new tower. In 1889, Congress authorized $40,000 to build a lighthouse in Carrabelle but postponed construction until 1894-1895.[10]

---

[10] Canetta, John , Speech to the Florida Lighthouse Association Quarterly Meeting, Carrabelle, Florida, January 2001.

Chapter Nine

The Saint Marks Lighthouse
Saint Marks, Florida

The Saint Marks Lighthouse was built in 1829 for $11,765. The finished tower was not accepted because the tower walls were found to be hollow rather than solid as required. Contractor Calvin Knowlton reconstructed the tower in 1831 and later built a new tower in 1842, when the soil began eroding away from underneath the first tower.

The tower is 60 feet high sitting on a base 12 feet deep made of limestone blocks taken from the ruins of old Fort San Marcos de Apalache. The walls of the tower are four feet thick at the base and taper to about 15 inches at the top. The original light was a brass lamp but now the light is electrically powered and is seen about 15 miles on a clear evening. During the Civil War, federal troops blockaded the Apalachee Bay beyond the lighthouse and stray shells hit the tower and dwelling burning the woodwork.

The first keeper was Samuel Crosby in 1830 through 1839; followed by Benjamin Metcalf in 1839 through 1841. J. P. Mungerford was keeper during the hurricane of 1843, when huge waves covered the gulf coast near Saint Marks. The storm washed away every standing building except the tower. The Mungerford family survived by clinging to the garret floor of the tower but fifteen others whom had taken refuge in the dwelling drowned.

Mr. Charles Fine was appointed keeper in 1892 and twelve years later, his wife took over the duties. One of their daughters was born, reared and married in the lighthouse. She and her husband, J. Y. Gresham, were the best known of all the lighthouse dwellers. Mr. and Mrs. Gresham and their eight children witnessed the creation of the Saint Marks Migratory Bird Refuge in 1957. In 1960, the lighthouse was automated, triggered by an electric eye, at present, the U. S. Coast Guard maintains the light and the Refuge staff maintains the house and grounds.

U.S. Coast Guard Archives
Ca. 1867

Florida State Archives
Ca. 1914

Chapter Ten

A Collection of True Stories I Love To Tell

This edition is a collection of true short stories and yarns about living in lighthouses that I have loved telling my children and grandchildren.

I have always told my family that I was born at the Crooked River Lighthouse in Carrabelle, Florida. I really believed it to be true until I probated my parents' estate in 1979. During the probate process, I found my baby book among the possessions in my mother's cedar chest along with her prized valuables. The pictures and other information there revealed that I was born at the home of Mrs. Fannie Pickett in Carrabelle with Doctor A. E. Russell, attending physician. I was not born at the lighthouse as I always thought.

When I was two years old, my father transferred to the Cape Saint George Lighthouse on Little Saint George Island, Apalachicola, Florida. The island is a narrow barrier island that stretches for thirty miles or more. The island lies about two or three miles off the mainland of Florida's Gulf coast. Little Saint George Island widens into an elbow narrowing into a thin sliver of land at its western end. Known as Cape Saint George, the elbow is the site of a lighthouse erected in 1852. Big Saint George contains the land east of Little Saint George.

Upon Dad's assignment as assistant keeper, we lived in the assistant keeper's dwelling. This was a two-storied house with a brick lower floor and a frame upper floor. There were two bedrooms on the upper floor and one bedroom and a living room on the lower floor. The kitchen was separate from the living quarters connected by an open breezeway. In the kitchen was three-burner kerosene stove, sink (no running water), two pantries for foods and storage. Fireplaces provided heat in bedrooms and living room and heated the house.

The keepers were required to clean the station, paint the tower and buildings, record their daily activities and log the daily weather conditions. They also had to see that the oil lamps were filled, wicks trimmed and lens cleaned and polished every day. Life on the station could be filled with loneliness and monotony but the Lighthouse Service allowed married keepers to have their families live with him. In an effort to help keepers expand their minds, the Service provided the stations with small portable libraries of about fifty volumes; the books were shipped in cases "so constructed that they make a rather neat appearance when set upright on a table". The Service also required the keepers to record the air and water temperatures twice daily. This task was normally performed by the keeper or assistant but was assigned to Walter and me. At first, we did it as a task but later Dad paid us about 10 cents a week. One winter holiday, Mother designed a system to dip the bucket into the cold gulf water; she rigged a hook on the end of a long pole to keep our clothes and feet dry. Of course, we did not use the system in the summer months, too much fun getting wet!

Everything at the station had to be kept spic and span. We children helped to keep it that way as part of our being there; that is the way we were taught. A Lighthouse Service Inspector checked station quarterly. We always knew when he was coming because Dad always met him in Apalachicola and would bring him to the island on the lighthouse boat. That hour or so gave us a chance to find and clean any missed areas. When the inspector had completed his white glove inspection, Mother always fixed him a big meal, usually his favorite Apalachicola oysters, shrimp and crabs. Our favorite inspector, Commissioner Lamphier of New Orleans, usually brought us children some candies and a small toy. I think he was Dad's favorite, too.

There were no roads, automobiles nor any other convenience except an emergency telephone installed at the insistence of the Lighthouse Service. Our transportation was by horse and wagon and horseback. The station's water supply was kept in four cisterns; rainwater was captured by using gutters and down spouts on the two houses. We were the only family living on the island; the assistant keeper was a bachelor. During the years of the late 1920s and 1930s, we children had to entertain ourselves every day with the help of our parents.

Later, my parents bought a home in Apalachicola so we children could go to school. At that time, Walter III was the only child old enough to attend school. The house was large and roomy so Mother shared our home with her newly wed cousin, Emma Brooks and her new husband, Richard (Bunks) Porter during the late 1920s and early 1930s. Their first daughter, Emma Jo, was born at our 12th Street home on February 6, 1930. When I was four years old, my parents agreed that I could spend the winter months with Dad on the island for two years until I began my school days. As Dad and I took care of the lighthouse on the island, Mother lived in Apalachicola and took care of Walter and Betty.

He taught me how to fish; steer the lighthouse boat; harness the horse and wagon; how to steer the horse drawn wagon and to navigate the deep waters; how to read a compass and use the Apalachicola Bay beacons as guides. He taught me the real meanings of doing a job right the first time, the meaning of responsibility, truth and honesty.

He let me steer the boat on the days we "tended" the beacons. The four or five beacon lights burned kerosene and we fueled the beacons on a regular schedule. On days when the bay was calm, I would steer the boat to a beacon ladder; Dad would stand on the bow of the boat with a five-gallon kerosene can in the crook of his left elbow; he would climb the ladder and refuel the beacon as I circled the boat around until he signaled; then I steered the boat to the ladder and he would get back on board and on to the next beacon. I often steered the boat on our weekly supply trips to Apalachicola. We always docked the lighthouse boat at the Marks Brokerage Company pier along the

Apalachicola River waterfront. We always visited with Dad's friends, DeWitt, Homer and Aubrey Marks when we came to town for mail and supplies. Our friends, the Porters, nicknamed me "Cap'n" and that name stayed with me until I moved to Port Saint Joe as a teenager.

I helped Dad with the painting chores around the station, working on lights and boat repairs. I remember one cold day he was working in the boat on the lift and asked for a crescent wrench (my job was to pass out and collect the tools). I handed the wrench to him but the wrench slipped out of my hand and fell into the water. Being five years old; I became frightened as to what he might say or do but without hesitation, he removed his clothes, climbed down the ladder and jumped into the water and retrieved the tool. While drying off and putting on his clothes, he looked at me and said "No big deal". Those may not be his exact words but that that was the kind of person he was.

One of my daily tasks was to help Dad with preparing the lantern room each morning after he put out the light. He would wipe, clean and polish the lens and brass works and I would hang the curtains using a long pole with a hook gadget on the end to hold the curtain rings. The curtains were hung on three sides of the lantern room to keep the sunrays off the lens. The curtains were made of soft canvas material about three feet wide and six feet long and hung from wall hooks. I would remove the curtains at sundown, fold and store them in the lantern room until the next morning. We did not use curtains on the north side of the lantern room.

About 1930, Dad was appointed keeper of the Cape St. George Lighthouse and Mr. Thornton (Gus) Cooper was the new assistant keeper. We moved into the keeper's big house; what an improvement in space and living area, a porch all around the house, three bedrooms, large living room and fireplaces in every room and a detached kitchen across the breezeway. The kitchen was a large room with kerosene stove, running water in the sink (hand pumped from the cistern outside) and two large pantries. After a few years, Dad and Mr. Cooper bought kerosene refrigerators from the Sears Roebuck mail order catalogue. The two burners were lit every night to produce ice and a cold refrigerator. Those refrigerators were forerunners of gas/electric refrigerators now used in motor homes and trailers. We enjoyed iced tea, ice cream and cold drinks all summer in addition to increasing our time for food storage. No more eating all the fresh fish, oysters and other foods just to keep them from spoiling.

Our family friend, Neil Hinkley, owned a Shetland pony named "Prince". Around 1930, when the pony became a problem for the Hinkleys to board and keep, Neil's mother asked Dad to take Prince to St. George Island for us children to enjoy. She made arrangements to have Prince transported to the island on a friend's fish boat. Prince became a member of our animal family along with Neb, the lighthouse horse, Trixie, the German Shepard dog and Alice, the pig. Walter and I became fond of Prince; he was our constant riding companion along with Ole Neb. We often saddled the horses for an afternoon ride on the beach. Prince was very docile and loved to gallop; run in the surf, be petted and bathed. We decided that Prince should pull a wagon to ride the children. Dad and Mother bought a bright red wagon (unassembled) from the Montgomery Ward catalogue.

As Mr. Cooper and Dad assembled the wagon, Mother made a harness set to fit Prince. The wagon was a thing of beauty but, alas, we could not hitch Prince to the wagon. What could we do with a new red wagon? Dad suggested we could locate a goat on Sand Island (western end of St. George Island) to pull the wagon. We laughed and thought that was the funniest thing we had ever heard; a goat wagon! Well, Dad and I rode our horses to Sand Island to locate a goat. Dad told Trixie to find us a goat; well, she did. Trixie ran through the herd of wild goats and stopped beside a beautiful male goat with long curved horns. He did not move as Trixie stood beside him and Dad rode up to the goat and puts a rope around his horns and we started for home. The goat did not resist and followed us to the lighthouse. For two or three days, we petted, washed and fed the goat horse feed, corn and plenty of water. Dad and Mr. Cooper redesigned the harness to fit the goat and we were ready to ride. By now, I know you have guessed we named the goat "Billy".

In a few days, we decided it was time to test Billy with the wagon. That was the easiest thing we had to do; Billy acted as if he had always pulled a wagon. We did not use mouth bits on Billy but used a rope noose around his nose to control him. For several days, Dad would lead Billy pulling the wagon along the shore. Later, it was not necessary to lead Billy; he enjoyed his new job and pulled the wagon with the three riders nearly every afternoon. When our summer vacation days were almost over, Dad and I returned Billy to Sand Island to be with his friends for the winter months. At the start of the next summer's vacation days, we rode to Sand Island to see if we could find Billy and Trixie found him in the herd and went to him. He waited for Dad to put the rope around his horns and again followed us to the lighthouse. We had another summer of fun with Billy and the red wagon. We did this again every summer for several years and we had three or four summers of fun with Billy and the red wagon. Some people may find this story hard to believe but those of us that lived it, know it to be true.

On one of our afternoon rides, we found a black and white spotted piglet in one of our "caves". Our caves were scrub oak overgrown and bowed over to present a cave-like appearance. We searched the area for her mother but failed to find her. We brought the piglet to the lighthouse and took care of her. We named her "Alice" after a friend in Apalachicola, I am sure that Alice in Apalachicola did not know we used her name for our pig. Alice and Trixie followed closely behind the children all summer, waiting for the next escapade, to be fed or petted. I believe that Alice actually thought she was a dog! Alice stayed with us all that summer and Dad cared for her during the winter. Some months later, Alice came home with a litter of her babies; we adopted them, too. We appropriately named every one for members of Alice's family in Apalachicola. We three children often explored the island beaches for miles in each direction of the lighthouse. Each explorer pulled a homemade wagon containing food, water and Mother's goodies. Of course, Trixie and Alice were our walking companions.

One afternoon, Walter and I decided to go camping in one of our caves. We took Trixie and Alice to a cave not far from the lighthouse. We had our camping gear, food, water, bedrolls and all the stuff necessary to camp. After tiring from playing with Trixie and Alice, walking on the beach in the dark and eating supper, we retired for the night. Walter arose from his bedroll after what seemed as hours and built a campfire. He began preparing breakfast of bacon, eggs and coffee. I thought it was too early but he said the sun was coming up and he was hungry. As we were eating breakfast, we heard Trixie barking and noises on the beach! Dad on horseback rode up to the cave and said Mother was worried about us and wanted us to come home. Walter told Dad that we hadn't finished our breakfast and Dad replied "All right, finish your breakfast and come on home, your mother is concerned about you two". We finished our breakfast and went home. The clock on the mantle told us it was 10:00 P. M.

Walter and I had miniature sail boats, rigged to sail in a large pond on the beach. We set the rudders to allow the boats to sail to the other side of the pond and we would race around and reset the rudders for a return visit. I still have my boat. "The Sea Queen" is in storage and needs repairs, re-rigging and maintenance. The Sea Queen is still alive! Later, Dad and Mr. Cooper built us a real sailboat. It was a real beauty, red sails, centerboard and rudder. We kept the boat at the pier on the bay side at the lighthouse pier. We sailed the boat often and especially when Dad went to town, we would sail for several hours until he landed.

One of our tasks was to hitch the horse/wagon and take Dad to the bay side to the boathouse on days he went to Apalachicola for supplies and mail. He always telephoned before he left town so we could be at the pier to meet him. Sometimes, we left a little early to do some fishing, sailing or crabbing. Walter and I had great times together.

During the years of the late 1920s and 1930s we children had to entertain ourselves every day with the help of our parents, as there was no other family living on Saint George Island during our growing up period. My family entertained us with special outings, fish fries and games; on days a fish fry was scheduled, Dad and I would load the wagon with cast nets, old shoes, hats and buckets. My brother would drive us in the wagon to the Gap, a wide level spot; about two-three miles from the lighthouse toward Big Saint George. He would deposit us and return to the lighthouse to collect the fish fry goodies, Mother and Betty while Dad and I were catching the fish, usually mullet in the shallow waters around the Gap. When we had enough fish, we cleaned the fish, gathered wood and old bricks to make a fire rack to hold a blackened iron Dutch oven to fry the fish. When Mother, Betty and Walter arrived, we were ready to start the family fun. We always had plenty of fish, fries and all the goodies Mother brought. After dinner, we played games and told stories. What exciting times we had!

My Mother staged the most popular of all the games we played at the lighthouse called "Hocus Pocus". She would arrange for each child to enter a dark stand up closet containing a large hamper covered with a clean white sheet. The person would stand in front of the hamper waving his hands like a magician over the hamper while saying the words "hocus pocus, diamond ocus" three times. The magician would remove the white sheet to discover a nice surprise, usually an apple, orange, candy or a small gift. Mother arranged the game so that every child got a different gift. How did she do that? I remember in one game all three of us found white painter caps under the sheet and we wore those caps every day. The game was so popular with all of our young guests; they wanted to play often. My grown-up cousins still talk about "hocus pocus" every time we meet.

In 1938, Dad was assigned as keeper at the St. Joseph Point Rear Range Light in Port Saint Joe, Florida, known locally as the Beacon Hill Lighthouse. This lighthouse had all modern facilities, e.g., running water, bathroom, electricity, telephone and an icebox. The iceman came every day to refill the icebox.

This was indeed a plum of a job for our Dad. We were only ten miles from town on a paved road! The only beacon was at the end of a 600-foot walkway near the highway. Dad did not have to attend beacons in the bay or gulf. Although this lighthouse was really a beauty, I never felt I was living in a lighthouse here; the lighthouse had no boats, beacons or pier on the beach. The paved road was too close for a remote and romantic lighthouse site!

The U. S. Coast Guard assumed custody of lighthouses, beacons and aids to navigation in 1939. When the Coast Guard informed Dad that a photographer was coming to take an official picture of the lighthouse, he set tasks for all of us to do; rake yards, pick up trash, paint fences, buildings, etc. The station had to be spic and span for the picture taking. All of his tasks were completed and the official picture was made; lo and behold, someone forgot to close a gate!

Of course, Dad assigned tasks here, too. I remember that one of my daily tasks was to empty the icebox drain tray. It was fun for a while but it became a chore, emptying the drain tray into a pail and taking the pail of water down the stairs. Sometimes, I would forget to do this and the drain would flood the pantry. My job then was to mop and clean the pantry floor. There had to be a better way; I had a brilliant idea - - what if I put a hole in the floor, insert a hose in the drain tray and push the hose through the hole in the floor allowing the water to drain outside? I thought this was a magnificent feat so I did it. All went well until Dad spotted the water dripping under the lighthouse and called for an investigation. He finally approved my method and the icebox drained automatically for several years.

The lighthouse was deactivated in 1952 and the lighthouse was dismantled and moved to the Overstreet area. The lantern room fell and was destroyed during the dismantlement operation. Later in 1979, Danny Raffield of Port Saint Joe moved the lighthouse to Simmons Bayou and converted it into a private home.

In 1992, Mr. Raffield invited us to tour his restored lighthouse and was glad to show off his excellent restoration. I was surprised to see that he had restored the lighthouse as I had remembered it. The exterior was restored according to original blueprints but he had made interior changes to fit his needs. He had salvaged lumber, trim and flooring and marked and numbered each piece as to replace it in its original position.

Chapter Eleven

Thumbnail Sketches Of The Keepers

Walter Andrew Roberts, Sr.

The Beginning

The First Generation Dedication Starts Here...

Terms Of Service

June 13, 1894	August 20, 1902	1st Asst. Keeper	Cape St. George Lighthouse
August 30, 1902	April 10,1909	Keeper	Cape San Blas Lighthouse
April 16, 1909	1912	1st Asst. Keeper	Cape St. George Lighthouse

For generations past, our families have been tied to the sea. Way back in the 1700s, relatives were plying their trades as sailors, captains and seafaring people in and around Key West and the Bahamas.

Our first connection with the manning of lighthouses befell to my grandfather, Walter Andrew Roberts, Senior Walter was born in Key West, Florida on February 22, 1871; his father, William C. Roberts, was a seaman sailing the Atlantic Ocean and the Gulf of Mexico and his mother, Ann Elizabeth Archer, was the daughter of Benjamin Archer, Jr., a local blacksmith, son of Benjamin Archer, Sr., plantation owner in the Bahamas. On June 13, 1894, Walter Andrew Roberts, Senior, was appointed 1st Assistant Keeper at the Cape St. George Lighthouse, Apalachicola, Florida, and trimmed his first wick at the age of 23 years.

Keeper Edward G. Porter bought property and built a cottage on St. George Island and hired Miss Ola Rhodes to teach a school. Ten students, of whom six were members of his family and the other four children were children of Walter Roberts, the assistant keeper. Walter married Ada Florence McNeil, daughter of John B. and Emily Louise McNeil of Apalachicola, Florida. Walter and Ada Florence were parents of five children:

Myra Roberts	b. 1894	d.
Walter Andrew Roberts, Jr.	b. 1896	d. 1977
Claude John Roberts	b. 1899	d. 1918
Maude Roberts	b. 1904	d.
Minnie Roberts	b. 1912	d. 1966

Walter served as assistant keeper at Cape Saint George Lighthouse with Keeper Edward G. Porter from June 13, 1894 until August 30, 1902, when he transferred to Cape San Blas Lighthouse near Port Saint Joe and served as keeper at the lighthouse for seven years. On April 16, 1909, he returned to Cape St. George Lighthouse as 1st Assistant Keeper and served until his retirement in 1912. In her 1984 autobiography, Pearl Porter Marshall stated that Walter, after his retirement, operated a meat market for the Porter family in Apalachicola. Later, he was employed by the post office in Apalachicola until his death on August 14, 1932. Grandfather Roberts was buried in Magnolia Cemetery. Grandmother Roberts died in Apalachicola on November 5, 1946, and was buried beside grandfather.

Walter Andrew Roberts, Jr.

The Second Generation Dedication Starts Here

Terms Of Service

1919 - 1921	2nd Assistant Keeper	Pensacola Lighthouse, Pensacola, FL
1921 - 1925	1st Assistant Keeper	Crooked River Lighthouse, Carrabelle, FL
1925 -1931	1st Assistant Keeper	Cape St. George Lighthouse, Apalachicola, FL
1931 - 1938	Keeper	Cape St. George Lighthouse, Apalachicola, FL
1938 –1952	Keeper	St. Joseph Point Rear Range Light, Port St. Joe, FL

Walter Andrew Roberts, Jr. was born in Apalachicola, Florida, on February 29, 1896 while his father was serving as Assistant Keeper at Cape St. George Lighthouse on Saint George Island.

He was called "Pete Roberts" in Apalachicola, Port Saint Joe, Carrabelle and the by lighthouse keepers who knew him. Although the name was tacked on during his childhood years, it stayed with him throughout his adult years. My mother, however, used his given name "Walter" and I recall "Walter" being used on formal occasions and by those who didn't know him very well.

On May 31,1916, Walter enlisted in the United States Army in Apalachicola and went overseas to France on October 6, 1916 during World War I; he served with the Medical Corps as an ambulance driver and medic in France until June 25, 1919. He returned to the United

States on July 6, 1919 and was discharged from the army on July 15, 1919, at the Medical Base Hospital #90, Camp Gordon, Georgia.

Walter Andrew Roberts, Jr., entered the United States Lighthouse Service in 1919, following in his father's footsteps. Walter was assigned as assistant keeper at the Pensacola Lighthouse and he, too, trimmed his first wick at the age of 23 years as his father.

With the beginning of World War I and after graduating from the Santa Rosa Academy in Mary Esther, Bessie went to work in the Pensacola Post Office. Bessie was a member of the Pryor and Rogers founding families and developers of Pensacola and Mary Esther. On Thanksgiving Day in 1919, she visited her cousin, Emma Pryor Brooks and her husband, Keeper Clem Brooks, at the Pensacola Lighthouse for dinner and a family get-together. There she met Walter Roberts on his first assignment with the U. S. Lighthouse Service, following in his father's footsteps.

Walter married Bessie Pryor at the Pensacola home of a relative on October 10, 1920. After their marriage, they lived in the Gulf Coast towns of Pensacola, Carrabelle, Apalachicola and Port Saint Joe.

They had four children:

Walter Andrew Roberts III b. August 3, 1921   d. February 18, 1961
William Claude Roberts   b. July 3, 1923
Elizabeth Aileen Roberts b. August 30, 1925
Evelyn Janice Roberts   b. March 6, 1934

In 1921, Walter transferred to the Crooked River Lighthouse in Carrabelle, Florida, as 1st Assistant Keeper and served from 1921 until 1925 under Keeper Thornwald Hansen. Keeper Hansen had replaced the retired keeper prior to Dad's arrival on station.

My brother, Walter A. Roberts III, was born on August 3, 1921, at Grandfather Roberts' house in Apalachicola while Dad was assistant keeper at Crooked River Lighthouse. My parents traveled by boat from the light station to Apalachicola, as there were no roads; the boat was their only contact with the outside world.

In July 1923, their second son, William was born and I have always told my family and friends that I was born at the lighthouse; I really believed it to be true until I probated my parents' estate in 1979. During the proceedings, I found my baby book in Mother's hope chest, the notes and pictures indicated that I was born in Carrabelle at the home of Mrs. Frances Pickett. Mrs. Pickett and Dr. A. E. Russell were attending nurse and physician. I wasn't born at the lighthouse after all!

In 1925, Walter Andrew Roberts, Jr. transferred to Cape St. George Lighthouse, Apalachicola, Florida, as 1st Assistant Keeper. He moved into the assistant keeper's quarters, the same house he had lived in as a child when his father was assistant keeper under Keeper Porter. He had come home. Our sister, Elizabeth (Betty) was born in Apalachicola during our first years at Cape St. George Lighthouse.

Around 1925, my parents bought a home in Apalachicola so the children could go to school but at that time, Walter was the only child old enough to attend school. When I was four years old, my parents agreed I could spend the next two years on St. George Island with my father until I was old enough to attend school. As Dad and I took care of the lighthouse on the island, Mother took care of her two children in Apalachicola; they spend holidays and every summer with us on the island.

Dad was appointed keeper in the early 1930s and we moved into the keeper's big house. Our second sister, Evelyn (Jan) was born in Apalachicola on March 6, 1934; now our family was complete.

Walter served as keeper at Cape St. George Lighthouse until June 30, 1938 when he was assigned to the St. Joseph Point Rear Range Lighthouse in Port Saint Joe, Florida.

Walter Andrew Roberts, Jr. arrived at the St. Joseph Point Rear Range Light Station on June 30, 1938, to relieve retiring Keeper Thomas Clarman (Clem) Brooks. Dad was to be the third and last keeper of this Gulf Coast station. Keeper Charles Lupton had served for 26 years when he retired in 1928 then came Keeper Clem Brooks for ten years; followed by Keeper Walter Roberts in 1938.

In 1939, the United States Coast Guard assumed command of all lighthouses, beacons and aids to navigation. Dad had three options, one option was to retire; remain as a civilian and the third option was enlistment in the Coast Guard. He opted for enlistment in the Coast Guard as Chief Petty Officer and served for 13 years

Walter retired from the Coast Guard when the station deactivated in 1952. He remained on station for approximately 10 months as a civilian custodian pending disposal of government equipment and property. In 1953, Walter and Bessie moved to Mary Esther, Florida.

Following retirement, Walter worked eight years for an electronics company at Eglin Air Force Base, Florida, and retired for a second time. Later, he worked at the Mary Esther Post Office for fourteen years, again following in the footsteps of his father.

Walter Andrew Roberts, Jr. died in the West Florida Medical Center, Pensacola, Florida, on October 3, 1977, and was buried in Jesse Rogers Cemetery, Mary Esther, Florida. Bessie Pryor Roberts died in Fort Walton Beach, Florida, on February 7, 1978, and was buried beside Walter in the Jesse Rogers Cemetery, Mary Esther.

Walter Andrew Roberts III

The Third Generation Dedication Starts Here…
Another Walter Roberts Comes Home!

Term Of Service:

1941 - 1945   Crooked River Lighthouse, Carrabelle, Florida

Walter Andrew Roberts III was born in Apalachicola in 1921 and lived at the Crooked River Lighthouse until 1925 while his father was 1st Assistant Keeper there. In 1941, he enlisted in the U. S. Coast Guard in New Orleans and after basic training; he received his assignment to the Crooked River Lighthouse and served on station for about four years. He had come home, too, following in the footsteps of his father.

Walter married Madeline Soderberg of Port Saint Joe and they had one son, Walter Arthur Roberts, born in Jacksonville, Florida, on February 11, 1948.

Walter Andrew Roberts III died in Jacksonville, Florida, on February 18, 1961 and was buried in Jesse Rogers Cemetery, Mary Esther, Florida. Madeline Soderberg Roberts died in Jacksonville, Florida, in July 1998 and was buried beside Walter in Jesse Rogers Cemetery, Mary Esther.

About the Author

William was born in Carrabelle, Florida, while his father was an assistant keeper at the Crooked River Lighthouse. He has lived on lighthouse stations for over twenty-five years and attended local Florida schools in Apalachicola and Port Saint Joe; graduated from the Florida State University in 1950. While serving his company as contract administrator, he enrolled in the Florida State University Graduate School and is the author of two technical documents submitted to the graduate school as partial fulfillment of the MBA degree program. Additionally, he authored several labor and cost savings documents along with many management procedures that are currently being used by his company.

He retired from his company after 35 years service as an accountant, contract administrator and senior contracts manager and lives in Mary Esther, Florida, with his wife of 57 years, Verner Mahon Roberts. They have four children, five grandchildren and two great-grandchildren.

Bill is a member of the United States Lighthouse Society, Florida Lighthouse Association and the Carrabelle Lighthouse Association. He has devoted time and energy to help these associations obtain funds and grants for restoration of lighthouse facilities.

He is a lighthouse historian and storyteller and has presented his lighthouse lecture series to numerous historical societies, churches, universities and interested organizations throughout Northwest and North Florida.

William C. Roberts
118 Point Comfort Road , Mary Esther, FL 32569
(850) 243-3797)   billroberts118@cox.net

LaVergne, TN USA
12 November 2010
204596LV00005B/3/A